I0880964

salmonpoetry

Publishing Irish & International

Poetry Since 1981

the weight of dandelions

Peter J. Gloviczki

Published in 2019 by
Salmon Poetry
Cliffs of Moher, County Clare, Ireland
Website: www.salmonpoetry.com
Email: info@salmonpoetry.com

ISBN 978-1-912561-61-2

Cover Design & Typesetting: *Siobhán Hutson*

Printed in Ireland by Sprint Print

Salmon Poetry gratefully acknowledges the support of
The Arts Council / An Chomhairle Ealaíon

Acknowledgments

The author wishes to gratefully acknowledge the following publications, in which certain of these poems (sometimes in earlier versions and with different titles) first appeared:

Acorn, Contemporary Haibun Online, DailyHaiku, elimae, Frogpond, Margie, Modern Haiku, The Christian Science Monitor, The Orange Room Review, The Rochester (Minnesota) Post Bulletin, tinywords, 3Lights.

Contents

I

clear night . . .
the radio brings
our team home

after the dance . . .
just the moon
to chaperone

late September . . .
I tighten the cap
on the sunblock

driving away . . .
we mouth
good-bye

back home . . .
digging the key
out of the plant

autumn evening . . .
carving the pumpkin
all by myself

holiday cards . . .
merry this
and happy that

flurries . . .
adding brandy
to my nightcap

late morning . . .
the coffee mug
in my left hand

December snowstorm:
our backyard branches
gaining holiday weight

she asks
how I take my gin:
evening rain

II

spring thaw . . .
collecting the hat
I loaned to Frosty

evening snow . . .
not sure
what day it is

job interview . . .
the weight
of Dad's belt

evening wind . . .
all the things
we couldn't carry

queen-size bed:
the dog lets me
sleep there too

late Spring . . .
leaving my coat
there on its hook

camping trip . . .
a crowd of stars
against our tent

everyone asks Him
for the same thing
—morning prayer

August breeze . . .
inviting ourselves
to the barbecue

along the shore . . .
the few rocks
we didn't skip

visit home . . .
a new fish
in the pond

five-thirty . . .
the birds
awake too

rummage sale . . .
combing her dolls
for the last time

at the wall . . .
learning her
given name

sweater morning . . .
cinnamon floats
in hot chocolate

early snow . . .
the last leaf
turns white

the funeral . . .
I read the verse
you read to me

visiting his grave . . .
as always
he listens

deer hunting . . .
I wear the vest
my father wore

class reunion . . .
remembering
who we were

broken umbrella:
His side
not ours

Christmas shopping—
the revolving door
here not here

evening frost . . .
putting the scraper
in the glovebox

below freezing . . .
only the stars
remain outside

the frayed edges of her picture—
I grasp what my fingers remember

Valentine's Day . . .
buying myself
dark chocolate

March evening . . .
just enough rain
to fall asleep to

on tip-toes
trying
not to wake you

Spring day . . .
flowers
I've never seen

late April . . .
somewhere
birdsong

brisk wind . . .
recognizing
her perfume

catching up . . .
smoke rings
on the porch

borrowed time . . .
leaving a nickel
in the change slot

economic news:
i wonder
will this jacket
be enough

III

in the breeze . . .
the weight
of dandelions

evening sun . . .
the steady pace
of the tire swing

late July . . .
two fireflies
trading light

evening rain . . .
how quickly the
birdbath
overflows

summer heat:
even the dog
in the shade

at the nightclub:
squad cars pass
lights and music

reunion concert . . .
performing the way
she used to sing it

tracing a box
for two . . . I flirt
with the mime

funeral for coach—
whistle on the coffin
first time off his lips

the wake . . .
teaching my son
a Windsor knot

bright morning . . .
even up there
you remember

the weight
of an empty field
is measured
by the voice
it carries . . .

homecoming:
I ask a stranger
for directions

PETER J GLOVICZKI is the author of *Kicking Gravity* (Salmon Poetry, 2013) and *American Paprika* (Salmon Poetry, 2016). *the weight of dandelions* is his third collection of poetry. His poems have appeared in *Beloit Poetry Journal*, *Hayden's Ferry Review*, *New Orleans Review*, *The Christian Science Monitor* and elsewhere. His work has also been anthologized in *Dogs Singing: A Tribute Anthology*. Born and raised in Rochester, Minnesota, he holds a BA from St. Olaf College and an MA and PhD from the School of Journalism and Mass Communication at the University of Minnesota. He works as an assistant professor of communication at Coker College in Hartsville, South Carolina, USA.

salmonpoetry

Cliffs of Moher, County Clare, Ireland

"Like the sea-run Steelhead salmon that thrashes upstream to its spawning ground, then instead of dying, returns to the sea—Salmon Poetry Press brings precious cargo to both Ireland and America in the poetry it publishes, then carries that select work to its readership against incalculable odds."

TESS GALLAGHER